HUMANS AND OUR PLANET

HUMANS AND OTHER LIFE ON EARTH

Sharing the Planet

by Ava Sawyer

CAPSTONE PRESS
a capstone imprint

Fact Finders Books are published by Capstone Press,
1710 Roe Crest Drive, North Mankato, Minnesota 56003
www.mycapstone.com

Library of Congress Cataloging-in-Publication Data
Library of Congress Cataloging-in-Publication data is available on the Library of Congress website.

ISBN 978-1-5157-7197-5 (hardcover)
ISBN 978-1-5157-7211-8 (paperback)
ISBN 978-1-5157-7215-6 (eBook PDF)

Humans have influenced the world around them since they first walked on Earth. Hunting has impacted animal populations. Pollution and deforestation have affected habitats. Humans have also worked to protect the environment through animal preserves and breeding programs. Learn about both the positive and negative impacts humans have on the planet.

Editorial Credits
Editor: Nikki Potts
Designer: Philippa Jenkins
Media Researcher: Jo Miller
Production Specialist: Kathy McColley

Photo Credits
Newscom: EPA/Barbara Walton, 23, EPA/Rungroj Yongrit, 25, KRT/Rick Martin, 24, Minden Pictures/Cyril Ruoso, 22; Shutterstock: a katz, 26, airphoto.gr, 18, Alexander Mazurkevih, 14, creativestockexchange, 4, (middle), Damix, cover, Designua, 5, Edgar Bullon, 6, Heiko Kiera, 17, ieang, 15, Igor Janicek, 4, (right), Imagentle, 4, (bottom), Kateryna Kon, 4, (top left), klublu, 4, (top right), miropink, 4, (left), Paulo Vilela, 16, Pete Niesen, 21, Rawpixel.com, throughout (background), Richard Whitcombe, 13, rismithtx, 11, Svetlana Foote, 9, Travel_Master, 10, William Silver, 20, XiXinXing, 27

Printed and bound in China.
004655

TABLE OF CONTENTS

CHAPTER 1
WHAT IS THE BIOSPHERE?

Human beings are part of the biosphere. The biosphere includes all living things and the areas on and around Earth where they can be found. Living things include plants, animals, fungi, and other small organisms, such as bacteria.

bacteria

people

THE BIOSPHERE

fungi

animals

plants

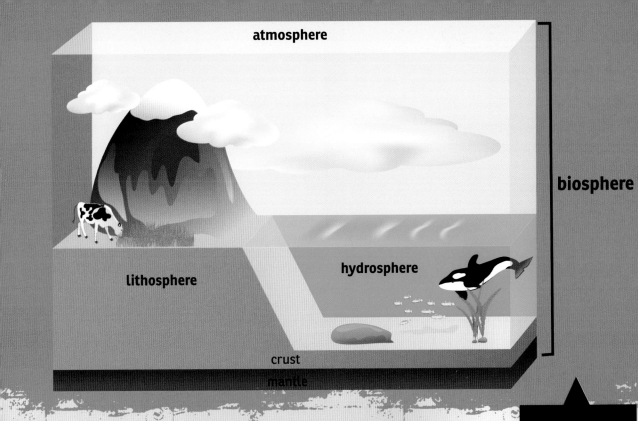

The biosphere extends into deep ocean trenches where tiny organisms live. It also stretches high up into the air where birds soar. It includes all of Earth's different **habitats**. All organisms need certain things to live. They need energy, nutrients, the proper temperature, and moisture. All of these necessities of life can be found within the biosphere.

Extending from the deepest part of the living ocean up to the highest part of the sky, the biosphere is about 12 miles (19 kilometers) tall. Because living things are always changing, the range of the biosphere is constantly changing as well. If a bird suddenly began to fly higher than before, the biosphere would stretch to include that bird's new flight pattern.

The biosphere overlaps with Earth's other spheres: hydrosphere, atmosphere, and lithosphere.

habitat—the natural place and conditions in which a plant or animal lives

CHAPTER 2
HUMAN INFLUENCE

Things that threaten plant and animal species come in many forms. However, one common factor is people. Human development often threatens to a living thing's ability to survive in nature. For about the last 100,000 years, humans have been the most dominant creatures on the planet.

People have developed tools to help them hunt and kill animals. They have learned to survive and live in almost every habitat on Earth. They have built technologies that spew pollutants into the air and dump waste into the world's waterways. Humans are having a great effect on the planet and all of its many species.

Human development has overtaken many habitats and displaced the animals that once lived there.

HUNTING

People mostly hunt wild animals for food. But in most cases animal populations have not grown as quickly as people's needs. This puts stress on certain living things. For example, some cultures eat sea turtles and their eggs. All but one sea turtle species is now considered **endangered**.

But not all animals have been hunted for food. In the 1800s American bison were shot for sport, not food. Millions were killed, and they were nearly hunted to **extinction**.

Some animals are hunted for their special features. These animals are often at high risk for extinction. Many elephants are killed for their ivory tusks, which have been used to make jewelry and piano keys. All species of elephants are considered endangered. Rhinoceroses have suffered a similar fate. Their horns have been used to make traditional medicines, as well as jewelry. All species of rhinoceroses are endangered. The West African black rhinoceros was declared extinct in 2011.

Extinction Events

In the past, there were some huge global catastrophes, such as extreme volcanic activity and asteroid strikes. When a large percentage of living things goes extinct over a short geological time — a few thousand to a few million years — it is called a mass extinction.

Some scientists think that we are entering a sixth mass extinction. Due to human impact, the rate of extinction has risen above the normal background rate. Instead of a few species going extinct every year, scientists estimate that a few are going extinct every day.

endangered—at risk of dying out

extinction—no longer existing

The Extinction of the Pyrenean Ibex

The Pyrenean Ibex was a species of wild mountain goat that lived in Europe. Human activities, such as hunting and clearing the land for livestock, caused the goat to become endangered. In 2000 the last surviving Pyrenean Ibex died and the species became extinct. Because living things depend upon one another as food sources, the endangerment or extinction of one organism can have a large impact on the entire biosphere.

More than 100,000 African elephants were illegally killed between 2010 and 2012.

POLLUTION

In the United States each person creates about 4 pounds (1.8 kilograms) of waste a day. That equals around 220 million tons (200 million metric tons) of trash a year. All that garbage has a negative effect on the environment. It can pollute the water where fish swim and poison the soil plants need to grow.

Amphibians

Amphibians have moist, absorbent skin. This makes them especially vulnerable to pollutants. Runoff water from farmers' fields can be filled with **pesticides**. These poisons end up in the lakes, swamps, and rivers where frogs and salamanders live, causing them great harm. More than a third of all amphibians are listed as endangered.

When waste ends up in the environment, it can be easily found by animals. Items such as chemicals and plastics can be harmful to animals.

pesticide—a poisonous chemical used to kill insects, rats, and fungi that can damage plants

California condors

Some animals are more affected by pollution than others. DDT was a widely used pesticide in the mid-1900s. Although this poison was directed at insects, it traveled through the **food chain**. If an insect sprayed with DDT got eaten by a fish, then that fish would have DDT in its body. If an eagle ate that fish, then the DDT would get passed along to the eagle. The more fish with DDT the eagle ate, the more poison it would have in its system.

While DDT didn't directly kill the birds of **prey**, it caused them to lay eggs with shells that were too thin. Often, the eggs would break before the baby birds were ready to hatch, and they would die. The problem was so great it nearly pushed California condors to extinction. At one point, just over 20 of them existed in the wild.

food chain—a series of organisms in which each one in the series eats the one before it

prey—an animal hunted by another animal for food

CLIMATE CHANGE

Climate change is another possible effect of pollution. Many scientists claim that Earth's temperature is rising due to human activity. This warming puts stress on living things, including many plants and animals. For example, if there is a rise in temperature in an area, some plants that once populated the area might now find it difficult to grow there. Animals relying on those plants for food may then be at risk of starvation and need to **migrate**. **Predators** that feed on the plant-eating animals will then struggle to survive as their prey disappears.

Coral reefs are a good example of the negative effects of climate change. Overly warm water causes tiny coral-forming animals, called polyps, to die. But the effect goes beyond just polyps. Thousands of plant and animal species make their homes in and around coral reefs, which are incredibly diverse ecosystems. As the coral dies out, many other species are left without shelter and food. They too are then at risk.

In addition to rising water temperatures, increasing levels of carbon dioxide also damage coral reefs.

migrate—to move from one place to another at different times of the year

predator—an animal that hunts another animal for food

HABITAT DESTRUCTION

The biggest threat to plant and animal species comes from the destruction of their habitats. Forests have been cut down for farmland. Resorts have been built on sandy beaches. Loss of habitat is perhaps the number-one cause pushing living things to extinction. Unlike people, most animals cannot easily change habitats or find new sources of food.

With beachfront property being developed, sea turtles' nesting grounds are disturbed.

Palm oil seedlings sprout on a plantation in Thailand.

Other activities such as farming and building also put animals at risk. In Indonesia, forests are being burned down to farm palm oil trees. Sun bears, orangutans, and other animals that live in these forests are now considered endangered. The loss of habitat has put a lot of stress on their populations in the wild.

MOVEMENT

Human movement, or migration, also changes the biosphere. When people move to new areas, they often bring plants and animals along with them. Introducing living things into new habitats can change the **biodiversity** of a habitat. Biodiversity is the variety of living things found in an area. When humans bring new crops, such as corn, to an area, they change that area's biodiversity. Additionally, clearing land for corn to grow results in the loss of many types of plants that were previously there. In this way, the area has lost biodiversity.

Acres of land are cleared in Brazil for soybean fields.

biodiversity—variety of life in genetics, species, and ecosystems

Changes in habitat impact predators such as Burmese pythons as well as the plants and animals that are below them in the food chain.

A new crop can also disrupt the natural balance of an area. For example, a large field of wheat may provide many animals with a new food source. Birds, rabbits, and squirrels may eat the wheat and grow in population. Predators of these animals might enjoy this change because their own food source will increase as well.

However, not all living things benefit from this type of change. The plants that were formerly eaten by birds, squirrels, and rabbits may grow out of control. They could take valuable land space away from other plants. This change could affect other animals that depend on those plants.

CHAPTER 3

MODERN IMPACTS ON THE BIOSPHERE

Modern technology also has an enormous impact on the biosphere. Using fuel-powered machines allows humans to live nearly anywhere on the planet. Humans can survive in arctic temperatures thanks to heaters. People can live on houseboats on the ocean using boat engines. Devices like these allow people live in habitats that would otherwise be unsuitable for them. And when humans move into new habitats, they often displace other living things already there.

Strip mining clears large areas of land, displacing animals that once lived there.

Modern machines usually need an energy source to work. Humans often use **fossil fuels** such as coal, gas, and oil for energy. Using fossil fuels causes many indirect changes to the biosphere. Fossil fuels are usually found deep underground. They must be drilled or dug out with machines and pumps. This greatly changes the landscape and disrupts the behavior of living things in the area. Plants and animals are often displaced, injured, or even killed by workers digging for fuel.

FACT

Using fossil fuels also creates pollution. The process of finding, transporting, and burning fossil fuels leads to land, air, and water pollution. When these parts of the biosphere, hydrosphere, and atmosphere are polluted, living things can be harmed.

fossil fuel—natural fuel formed from the remains of plants and animals; coal, oil, and natural gas are fossil fuels

CHAPTER 4
PROTECTING THE BIOSPHERE

Not all human behavior is harmful to the biosphere. In fact, humans have done many things to help the biosphere. Governments, organizations, and eco-friendly businesses are all working to protect the biosphere in different ways.

Many organizations are trying to reverse some of the ways human behavior has harmed the biosphere. To lessen the negative impact of **deforestation**, environmental groups and eco-friendly businesses are encouraging people to replant trees. Replanting a large number of trees helps keep the soil in forests healthy. It also helps keep the atmosphere balanced.

FACT

Scientists working for energy companies are developing renewable fuel sources as alternatives to fossil fuels. They are looking at more efficient ways to use energy from the sun, wind, and water to fuel machines.

Signs help protect wildlife habitats by reminding people not to disturb native animals.

deforestation—to remove or cut down trees

PROTECTING HABITATS

One of the most common forms of **conservation** is establishing protected areas for plants and animals. In most cases, parks are set up to protect a wide range of species living in an area, as well as their habitat. Sometimes **sanctuaries** are established to help specific animals, especially those that are critically endangered.

Parks are not only on land. They can also be at sea. The Great Barrier Reef Marine Park is located off the northeastern coast of Australia. This reef is considered the largest **ecosystem** in the world. Being defined as a park allows workers the authority to oversee the fishing and shipping that happens within the park's boundaries. This helps protect the thousands of animal species that live in and around the reef.

Great Barrier
Reef Marine Park

conservation—the protection of animals and plants

sanctuary—a place where animals are cared for and protected

ecosystem—a system of living and nonliving things in an environment

CAPTIVE BREEDING PROGRAMS

In extreme cases, if a species population becomes too small in the wild, scientists set up a captive breeding program. They take animals from the wild and place them in zoos or other enclosures. These areas are similar to the animals' natural habitats. Males and females are then brought together to mate and reproduce young. The short-term goal is to prevent the species from becoming extinct. As more young are born and reach maturity, animals can be reintroduced to the wild.

FACT

The Sumatran Rhino Sanctuary was created in the Way Kambas National Park in Sumatra, Indonesia. The park consists of swamps and rain forests. It provides a protected area for endangered animals such as tapirs, tigers, elephants, and ducks.

Workers at Indonesia's Sumatran Rhino Sanctuary help care for and protect the Sumatran rhinoceros from poachers.

Two three-month-old clouded leopard cubs are raised at the world's first Clouded Leopard breeding center in Khao Kheow Open Zoo in Thailand.

A California condor is released in the Ventana Wilderness in California.

Pandas, clouded leopards, and maned wolves are some of the animals currently in captive breeding programs. But one of the most successful stories is that of the California condor. In the 1980s only 23 of these large birds were known to exist in the world. They were all captured and placed in a breeding program. The breeding program has been successful, and many condors have been released from **captivity**. Today several hundred condors live in the wild as a result of this successful program.

Although a few breeding programs have been successful, many fail. Reintroducing captive animals to the wild can be difficult. Captive animals need to be taught how to find food and shelter in the wild or they will not survive.

captivity—the condition of being held or trapped

INTERNATIONAL LAWS

Governments around the world have passed laws protecting endangered species. In the United States, the Endangered Species Act makes it illegal to hunt, collect, and destroy the habitat of certain animals. International laws make it illegal for people to hunt and kill animals such as whales, elephants, and rhinoceroses. The laws also make it illegal to buy and sell products from these animals.

A forensic police officer inspects smuggled African elephant tusks in Thailand.

CHAPTER 5

HOW CAN HUMANS HELP?

You don't have to work for the government or an environmental agency to help the biosphere. There are many small actions you can take every day to improve the condition of the environment. First, respect the natural world. Take care of waste properly. Only throw away what can't be recycled, composted, or reused. Do not throw batteries, paint, or oil in a trash bin. These items need to be taken to a facility that can properly dispose of the materials. Otherwise they can create harmful pollution.

People can also donate to wildlife organizations. There are many charity groups around the world that promote conservation efforts. They may set up animal hospitals, help establish parks, and even work to pass laws to protect certain plant and animal species. Visiting national, state, and municipal parks shows support for protected natural areas.

Properly disposing of garbage helps keep animal habitats free of pollution.

Trees and other plants are positive for the environment. Through natural processes, they release oxygen and take in carbon dioxide from the air.

People can even help out in their backyards. Growing flowers and other plants that provide food for insects such as butterflies and bumblebees will help increase their chances of survival. People can also set up bird feeders and nest boxes.

Lastly, tell your friends! Educate them about how humans can both negatively and positively impact the biosphere. When people know more about the outcome of their actions, they are more likely to change their behavior.

TIMELINE

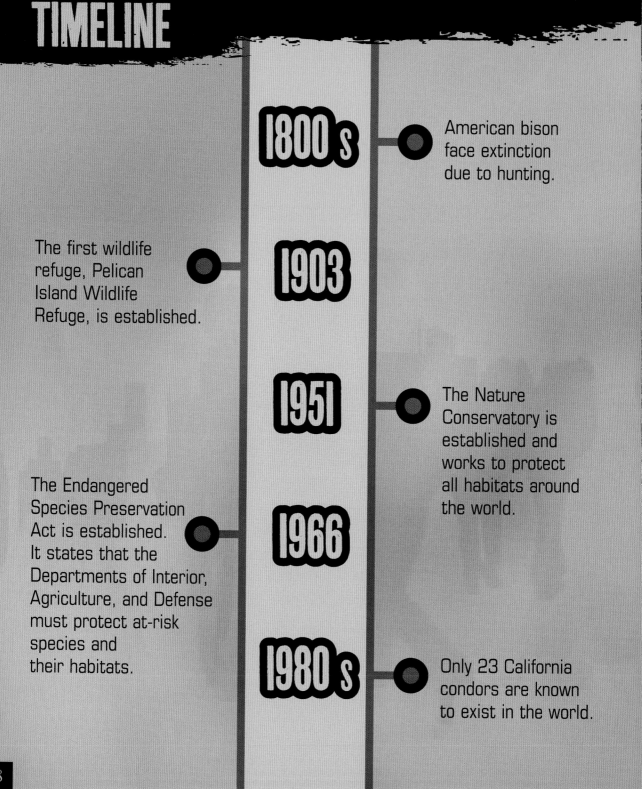

1800s — American bison face extinction due to hunting.

The first wildlife refuge, Pelican Island Wildlife Refuge, is established. — **1903**

1951 — The Nature Conservatory is established and works to protect all habitats around the world.

The Endangered Species Preservation Act is established. It states that the Departments of Interior, Agriculture, and Defense must protect at-risk species and their habitats. — **1966**

1980s — Only 23 California condors are known to exist in the world.

2000

SanWild Wildlife Trust is established. The Africa-based wildlife reserve works to protect animals and get them back to their lives in the wild.

2008

As Arctic sea ice continues to decline, polar bears are listed as threatened species under the Endangered Species Act.

2011

The West African black rhinoceros is declared extinct.

2012

The United Nations General Assembly (UNGA) declares March 21 International Day of Forests. The resolution encourages people to plant trees and organize events to promote awareness of the importance of forests.

GLOSSARY

biodiversity (bye-oh-duh-VUR-si-tee)—variety of life in genetics, species, and ecosystems

captivity (kap-TIV-i-tee)—the condition of being held or trapped

conservation (kon-sur-VAY-shuhn)—the protection of animals and plants

deforestation (dee-FOR-ist-ay-shuhn)—to remove or cut down trees

ecosystem (EE-koh-sis-tuhm)—a system of living and nonliving things in an environment

endangered (in-DAYN-juhrd)—at risk of dying out

extinction (ex-STINK-shun)—no longer existing

food chain (FOOD CHAYN)—a series of organisms in which each one in the series eats the one before it

fossil fuel (FAH-suhl FYOOL)—natural fuel formed from the remains of plants and animals; coal, oil, and natural gas are fossil fuels

habitat (HAB-uh-tat)—the natural place and conditions in which a plant or animal lives

migrate (MYE-grate)—to move from one place to another at different times of the year

pesticide (PES-tuh-side)—a poisonous chemical used to kill insects, rats, and fungi that can damage plants

predator (PRED-uh-tur)—an animal that hunts other animals for food

prey (PRAY)—an animal hunted by another animal for food

sanctuary (SANGK-choo-er-ee)—a place where animals are cared for and protected

READ MORE

Gogerly, Liz. *Caring for Animals*. Charities in Action. Chicago: Heinemann Library, 2013.

Iyer, Rani. *Endangered Energy: Investigating the Scarcity of Fossil Fuels*. Endangered Earth. North Mankato, Minn.: 2014.

Shea, Therese. *Overfishing*. Habitat Havoc. New York: Gareth Stevens, 2014.

INTERNET SITES

FactHound offers a safe, fun way to find Internet sites related to this book. All of the sites on FactHound have been researched by our staff.

Here's all you do:

Visit *www.facthound.com*

Type in this code: 9781515771975

Super-cool stuff!

Check out projects, games and lots more at
www.capstonekids.com

CRITICAL THINKING QUESTIONS

- What are some positive ways humans affect plants and animals? What are some negative ways?

- Hunting can lead to endangered animals and extinction. What is the difference between these two terms?

- Many animals, such as tigers, elephants, and California condors, are kept in captive breeding programs. What are captive breeding programs. How do these programs help endangered species recover?

INDEX